THE ORIGINAL
College Kid's Cookbook

by
Marion Hodgson

© 1967, 1968, 1974, 1976, & 1987
Copyrights by Marion Hodgson
ALL RIGHTS RESERVED

14th printing

ISBN 0-912848-01-4

College Kid's Cookbooks
624 North Bailey
Fort Worth
Texas
76107

TABLE OF CONTENTS

A not-in sequence

Necessities	4-5
MENUS	6-9

MAIN DISHES:

Here's what you Need for #1	10
QUICK CASSEROLE #1	11
Sea FOOD CASSEROLE	12
QUICK CASSEROLE #2	13
About Chicken	14
BaKeD OR BROILED CHICKEN	15
CHICKEN GRAVY	16
LEFTOVER SUGGESTIONS	17
HaRD BOILED EGGS	18
STEW	19
Here's what You Need for Meal-in-a-Skillet	20
Meal-in-a-Skillet (GOURMET)	21
Garlic Bread to go with	22
eaSY SPaGHETTi	23
TUNA SALAD SERVING SUGGESTIONS	24
TUNa SaLaD	25
Here's what you Need for	26
ROaST BeeF OR LamB	27

— continued —

Main Dishes (continued)

- Pot Roast — 28
- Steak — 29
- Turkey — 30
- One-Dish Meal "Meat Chowder" — 31
- Easy Pork Chops — 43

Vegetables

- Quick Vegetable Casserole — 32
- Green Beans — 33
- Baked Potatoes & Hints — 34 and 35
- Boiled Potatoes — 36
- Vegetable Soup — 44

HINT ABOUT VEGETABLES: Frozen vegetables that come in the little boiling bags are so easy to fix! Just follow directions on the package. (Simply boil water and drop the bag in for the specified time.)

Salads

- Bing Cherry Salad — 37
- Peach, Pineapple, Pear — 38
- Dressing (for above) — 38
- Cole Slaw — 39
- Tossed Green Salad — 40
- Basic Salad Dressing — 41
- Avocado & Mandarin Orange — 43

Quick Ambrosia — 42

→ First Shopping List & Keep In Stock List — 45 46 ←

Finger Foods & Dips — 47

Pork & Beans — 43

3

Necessities for the kitchen

The author is assuming that your apartment furnishes basic kitchen equipment: a can opener, dishes, etc. TAKE INVENTORY.

MAYBE SOME OF THESE THINGS ARE ALREADY FURNISHED

- Kettle for boiling water
- Large Teflon skillet & lid (YOU'LL COOK WHOLE MEALS IN IT)
- Two 2-qt. Teflon saucepans & lids
- Nylon spatula & spoons TO COOK WITH
- Casserole (or two)
- Teflon roast rack
- Tongs to lift things with (SURGICAL TONGS FROM A SURGICAL SUPPLY HOUSE ARE BEST.) You'll use these for everything from lifting hot drumsticks from the broiler to removing green beans from the saucepan.)
- Paper towels & holder
- Vegetable brush (Fuller's!)
- Aluminum foil (75 ft.)
- Wax paper
- Sponge
- Ring mold
- Colander
- Nylon baster →
- Teflon meat loaf pan

NECESSITIES

DID SOMEONE GIVE YOU THIS BOOK?

ASK 'EM TO ADD TO THIS LIST

- 1 one-quart Pyrex meas. cup
- Asbestos mitts or hot pads
- "Pam" to spray on nonTeflon pans
- Big strainer — FOR DRAINING FROZEN CHOPPED SPINACH, AFTER COOKING — ETC.
- Chopping board
- Juice shaker
- Meat thermometer (GET THIS AND BASTER AT DEPT. STORE IN KITCHENWARES SECTION)
- Pocket-size book on How to Carve
- Big glass cookie jar (SO YOU CAN SEE WHEN IT'S GETTING EMPTY)
- Blackboard & chalk (Pencils disappear) (WRITE THINGS DOWN BEFORE YOU RUN OUT)
- Pepper grinder
- Two big mixing bowls (ONE CAN DOUBLE AS SALAD BOWL)
- Teflon muffin tin (FOR EMERGENCY BISQUICK BISCUITS, ETC.)
- Big rubber gloves (EVEN A HE-MAN CAN'T STAND WATER THATS HOT)

MENUS

EVERYBODY'S FAVORITE:
- Steak p. 29
- Baked potatoes 35
- Tossed salad 40

Tuna Salad p. 25
- Quick vegetable casserole 32
- Corn muffins (buy frozen)

Meat Chowder
one-dish meal p. 31

Quick Casserole #2 p. 13
- Tossed green Salad 40
- (+ Dessert always optional)

Flounder Almondine — OR — Filet of Sole
Gorton's frozen (heat + eat)
- French-fried potatoes (buy frozen)
- Cole slaw (p. 39)

IN A PINCH (and delicious!):
GREEN PEA and HAM SOUP
With toast it's a meal. Takes 2-3 cans for 4 college kids. Add chunks of leftover ham, if you have any.

8

MENUS

Easy Spaghetti ㉓
Green Salad ㊵
Garlic Bread ㉒
Fruit

(Leg of Lamb ㉗
Boiled Potatoes ㊱
Mixed Vegetables (frozen))

Shrimp + Chicken Cantonese
(Stouffer's Lean Cuisine - frozen)
Whole Wheat Rolls (packaged)
Ambrosia ㊷

| Easy Pork Chops & Rice |
| Broccoli (frozen) |
| Avocado & Orange Salad ㊸ |

For a Party:
Meal-in-a-Skillet ㉑
Sourdough Rolls
(packaged)

A word about leftovers: Refrigerate them promptly (covered) in the same pan they were cooked in, when practical. Take out when ready to reheat, and use same casserole or pan for reheating. (Put casserole dishes in cold oven; then set heat.) This is the lazy man's way.

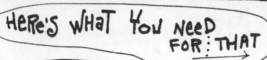

- Measuring cup & spoon
- Pkg. of MINUTE RICE
- Pan & lid
- Crisco Oil (or Wesson, etc.)
- <u>Large</u> Teflon frying pan (with or without lid)
- 2 lbs. ground meat (hamburger is okay)
- Empty can or carton for grease
  (to be hardened in refrig. & then thrown out)
- Salt
- Soy sauce
- Mushroom or Cheddar Cheese Soup

OPTIONAL:
for leftovers.
(They'll think it's a whole new dish!)--

  Onion
  Canned mushrooms
  Slivered almonds

AND A SPOON TO STIR WITH

You can also add grated cheese.

Quick "Casserole" #1

Only it's not really a casserole. You cook it in a frying pan!

ENOUGH FOR 4 TO EAT TWICE
(Use optional goodies*
    for second go-round.)

① Fix two cups - in pan - *(MEASURE WHEN UNCOOKED)* of **MINUTE RICE**, FOLLOWING DIRECTIONS ON BOX and put aside.

② Put 1 Tablespoon **CRISCO OIL** in skillet (TEFLON, hopefully) and PUT ON MED. HEAT. Then:

③ Dump in 2 lbs. **GROUND BEEF.** CHOP THE MEAT UP AS YOU STIR IT, AND TURN IT OVER AS IT BROWNS. DON'T OVERCOOK.

④ Pour off grease IN EMPTY CAN (SEE PAGE 10)

⑤ Add: 1 teaspoon **SALT**
          1 teaspoon **SOY SAUCE**
          1 can **MUSHROOM SOUP** (OR CHEDDAR CHEESE)

and heat through. When ready to serve,

⑥ Stir in cooked rice

*OPTIONAL INGREDIENTS (use one or all) WHICH CAN BE ADDED TO LEFTOVERS, to make them yummy:

Chopped onion, slivered almonds, mushrooms.
(Use almost any amount.)

Sea Food "Casserole" *ii

MIX TOGETHER:
- 1 Can each: (small)
  - LOBSTER
  - SHRIMP
  - CRABMEAT

When you feel like splurging

- 1 can Crab Soup (LIKE CROSSE & BLACKWELL MADRILENE)
- 1 can Mushrooms (ANY SIZE) (AS LARGE AS YOU CAN AFFORD)
- 1 can Cheddar Cheese Soup

Cook in 300-350° oven for 30 minutes*

STRETCH WITH HARD BOILED EGGS IF DESIRED

(This would probably be great made with frozen Cr. of Shrimp soup!)

SERVE OVER MINUTE RICE
(Directions & quantity on pkg.)

* Can be cooked in a saucepan Cook over MED. heat or slower.

Quick Casserole* #2
— Serves 4 —

- 2 cans boned **Chicken** (I use Swanson's)
- 1 can (Franco-American) **Macaroni & Cheese** (THERE'S ONLY ONE SIZE)
- ½ can undiluted **Cream of Chicken Soup**
- SPLASH OF MILK IF NEEDED
- Halves or slivers of **Almonds** or sliced-up **water chestnuts** (a palm full - to add crunchiness)

Bake in casserole dish in oven 300°-350° for 30 min.*

HINT: CAN SUBSTITUTE 1 CAN OF TUNA FOR CHICKEN — & CAN ALWAYS STRETCH WITH HARD-BOILED EGGS.

*or can be cooked in Teflon saucepan over MED. or LOW heat

(13)

about chicken...

Just about the easiest thing in the world to cook is chicken, because it can be cooked at almost any temperature for almost any length of time. If you cook it slow, but then decide to eat sooner than planned, simply move the chicken pan up higher in the oven underneath the broiler (or, if you have a separate broiler, put it there) -- and don't forget to set your stove on "BROIL": The chicken will brown quickly and be done in a flash, although you do have to turn it over, of course, if you broil it (which is not necessary when you bake it).

Chicken is done when it feels tender when stuck with a fork. Do brown it for appearance's sake, and never undercook chicken. It is difficult to overcook it in a slow oven, and if coated with undiluted cream of chicken (or mushroom) soup it need never be basted. Baked chicken makes mealtime flexible, which makes it a great party favorite. It can become almost a gourmet dish if you simply squeeze a little lemon juice over it while it's cooking (in which case, of course, you wouldn't use the soup!) But take it easy at first, and leave off the lemon altogether if you plan to use leftover chicken for creamed dishes.

A WORD OF WARNING ABOUT CHICKEN: Always keep it refrigerated. Wrap leftovers in foil and put in refrigerator immediately, even if chicken is still hot. Wash counter tops that raw chicken has touched.

LEFTOVER SUGGESTIONS: page 17

WHAT TO DO WITH GIBLETS: p. 17

Slow-baked chicken leaves lots of drippings in the pan. Save them (covered) in the refrigerator and use with leftovers or in GRAVY (page 16).

When you don't feel like cooking at all, bring home some Kentucky Fried Chicken!

(14)

Baked or Broiled Chicken

Buy fryer-size chickens already split in half. Cook enough for two meals while you're at it. **ECONOMICAL!**

① Wash chicken under running water.

② Put it in foil-lined pan (pretty side up, unless broiling).

③ Put pan in oven.

Slowest and best way: 250°. Can cook all afternoon without basting or turning.*

Fast way: 450° till tender when poked with a fork. Check in half an hour. It's best to rub chicken with butter first, when cooking fast.

Fastest way: BROIL. Set oven on "BROIL", or if you have a separate broiler, use it. Rub chicken skin with butter, and put chicken skin-side-down. It must be turned over at least once. Takes 15-20 minutes, total.

* Sensational when first coated with undiluted Cream of Chicken soup. Makes its own gravy! Just spoon the soup over top of chicken.

CHICKEN GRAVY

UNDILUTED CREAM OF CHICKEN SOUP MAKES GOOD GRAVY,

and with all the packaged gravy mixes on the grocer's shelf, there's no need to make gravy from scratch, unless you have extra time and want to use the good drippings (from the chickens you baked) -- which I hope you saved, covered, in the refrigerator.

IF SO, HERE'S HOW:

1) Heat <u>drippings</u> in pan. (MED. heat.)

2) Sprinkle in <u>flour</u>. (small amount, if you like thin gravy -- never more than the drippings) Always add flour to grease <u>before</u> adding liquid, and your gravy shouldn't be lumpy.

3) Simmer at least 10 min. so that gravy won't taste raw. Stir occasionally.

4) Add <u>liquid</u>, (water, milk, or stock. "Stock" is the water something was cooked in.) Stirring slowly, until gravy has the desired thickness.

5) Add <u>salt and pepper</u>. You can also add giblets (see opposite page) — or tiny pieces of leftover chicken, or hard-boiled eggs — or <u>all</u> of these things.

LEFTOVER SUGGESTIONS

CHICKEN

Creamed chicken over rice:—

CUT CHICKEN INTO HUNKS. ADD TO CHICKEN GRAVY (opposite page) OR TO CREAM OF CHICKEN SOUP, diluted with milk only as necessary to produce the thickness (or thinness) you desire.

YOU CAN ADD ANY OR ALL OF THESE IN ANY AMOUNT:
(Slice or Chop:)
- ALMONDS
- MUSHROOMS
- HARD BOILED EGGS
  (see next page for directions)

Serve over MINUTE RICE
(FOLLOW DIRECTIONS ON PACKAGE)

| Can also be served on toast |

FOR VARIATION, ADD CURRY POWDER TO TASTE

GIBLETS —Usually come with chicken. Wash under running water. Put in saucepan and cover with boiling (salted - ½ teaspoon) water and cover. COOK on LOW 15-30 min. Use water for stock for gravy. See opposite page for gravy recipe. CHOP UP COOKED GIBLETS AND ADD TO GRAVY OR CREAMED CHICKEN ON RICE.

HaRD-BoiLeD EGGS

USE SPARINGLY

See "Look Before You Leap" — inside front cover.

Shake: **SALT** (Tablespoon or more) into saucepan -- any kind, any size -- of **COLD WATER**. Fill pan half full.

Add: **EGGS** -- any number, in their shells, of course.

Bring water to rolling boil. BOIL GENTLY for 5 MINUTES,

then TURN BURNER OFF. LEAVE COVERED and leave alone for **half hour or more**.

In a hurry? Just boil 'em 20 minutes, instead.

<u>Cool</u> cooked eggs in ice water — or at least under running water.

This makes them easier to shell.

REFRIGERATE in shells till ready to use.

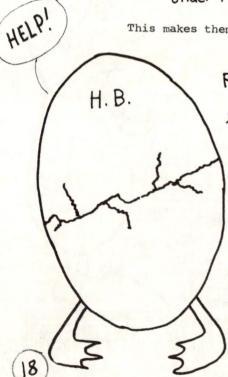

Hint: write "H.B." on eggs you store in refrigerator, so you won't mix 'em up with raw eggs.

STEW

GREAT WAY TO USE LEFTOVERS

Amount to buy depends on how many leftovers (meat and vegetables) you have to add to stew.

- **BUY:** 1 or 2 pkg. <u>frozen</u> stew vegetables, (Libby's or Ore-Ida are both good - 1½ lbs. ea.) containing potatoes, carrots, onions, & celery -
- **ALSO BUY:** 1 or 2 pkg. <u>LEAN stew meat</u> (1 or 2 lbs. NOT frozen - <u>cut into pieces</u>) HAVE KETTLE OF WATER BOILING.

QUICK METHOD:

- **Dump everything** (meat + froz. veg.) together into big Teflon saucepan. Add an inch or two of boiling water & 1½ teaspoon salt. LET BOIL GENTLY, AT LEAST ONE HOUR. Meat will be toughish*

ADD any leftover hunks of roast - or use leftover roast exclusively (Put it in at start.) Also dump in: any leftover vegetables that seem appropriate. I always add a few fresh carrots for more flavor and a quartered (fresh) potato or two, <u>when I have time</u>, because frozen potatoes disintegrate. But the vitamins are there, anyway, and the potatoes thicken the stew. IF IT NEEDS MORE THICKENING, add packaged brown gravy mix. (Kraft's is good. EXPERIMENT with McCormick's BEEF STEW SEASONING (comes in an envelope). It's good.

*Stew meat is more tender the longer it is cooked - so when you have time - put meat in first and cook as long as possible. ADD VEGETABLES LAST HOUR AND HALF.

Here's what you need
and what you need to do:
FOR THAT

- Large **frying pan** and lid
- Vegetable **oil** (Crisco, Wesson, etc.)
- 1 lb. **ground chuck** or round steak
  Buy this kind of LEAN ground meat for this recipe, since you won't be pouring off the grease this time (as you usually should.)
- Frozen chopped **onions**, or a fresh Bermuda onion
- Pkg. med. sized **noodles**
- (Med. size) Can of **tomato juice** or V-8
- **Salt**
- Black **pepper**
- **Celery** salt or a piece of celery
- **Worcestershire** sauce
- Frozen chopped **green peppers** or a fresh green pepper
- Small carton of **sour cream**
- 3-oz. can sliced **mushrooms**
- Measuring cup + spoons
- Can opener

> "Meal in a Skillet" is good served with canned green beans and French bread to round out meal without more work!

20

GOURMET

Meal in a Skillet

(GROUND BEEF IN SOUR CREAM)
Serves 4 - 6

- Put 1 Tablespoon of **veg. oil** in frying pan. Heat on MEDIUM.

- Dump in: 1 pound of **ground beef**

- Add: 1 cup (or less) of chopped **onion**

    COOK TILL TENDER BUT NOT BROWN.

- Dump on top: 3 cups of **raw noodles**

- Pour on top of that:

    - 3 cups **tomato juice or V-8**
    - 1 teaspoon **salt**
    - 1-1/2 teaspoons **celery salt**, or chop up a piece of celery
    - dash of **pepper**
    - 2 teaspoons **Worcestershire sauce**

- BRING TO BOIL. Turn heat down. COVER PAN AND SIMMER (on lowest heat) 20 minutes.

- Then add: 1/2 cup chopped **green pepper**

    COVER AND CONTINUE COOKING 10 MINUTES, or until noodles are tender.

- Stir in: 1 cup **sour cream**

    2/3 cup sliced **mushrooms** (drained)

- HEAT JUST TO BOILING.

Garlic Bread

For quick <u>garlic "butter,"</u> sprinkle tub of Chiffon (or other soft margarine made from safflower or corn oil) with garlic salt (easy does it! DON'T USE MUCH!) and mix.

Slice loaf of <u>French bread</u> in thick slices, BUT DON'T CUT QUITE ALL THE WAY THROUGH TO THE BOTTOM. Open between slices and spread with garlic "butter." Wrap in foil and heat in hot oven 425° for 10-15 minutes.

IF BREAD NEEDS BROWNING, DON'T WRAP TILL BROWN.

easy Spaghetti:

for 4

① Put: **1 Tbsp. Corn Oil** in large (Teflon) skillet on MED. HEAT

② Add: **½ to 1 Onion** - chopped up - cook a few minutes but no need to brown.

③ Dump in: **1½ lb. ground meat** Chop it up & turn it over till it's cooked through.

④ POUR OFF GREASE into old can for discarding

⑤ Add to contents in skillet:
- 1 large can Franco-Amer. <u>spaghetti</u>
- 1 (15 oz.) can <u>Kidney beans</u>
- 1 small bottle (or less) <u>Ketchup</u>
- ½ teasp. <u>Salt</u>

HEAT & MIX AND IT'S READY!

Add salad and hot (garlic?) bread and you have a meal!

SEE OPPOSITE PAGE

TUNA SALAD SERVING SUGGESTIONS

Tuna salad is good piled inside half an avacado (peeled) surrounded by lettuce leaves, (washed!)

ALSO GOOD STUFFED INTO A "FLOWERED" TOMATO - which is a (washed) tomato cut as shown below:

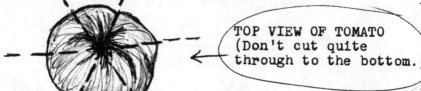

TOP VIEW OF TOMATO (Don't cut quite through to the bottom.)

After slicing as above, remove woody center and open sections outward into "flower" -- then pile tuna salad in center.

Open tomato as shown. This makes an individual serving.

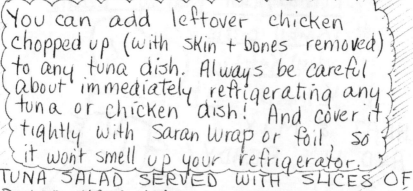

You can add leftover chicken chopped up (with skin + bones removed) to any tuna dish. Always be careful about immediately refrigerating any tuna or chicken dish! And cover it tightly with Saran Wrap or foil, so it won't smell up your refrigerator.

TUNA SALAD SERVED WITH SLICES OF BOILED HAM MAKES A GREAT ENTREE FOR A BUFFET SUPPER.

Tuna Salad

BEFORE YOU START: Do you have any hard-boiled eggs on hand? Not essential, but good in this. (SEE PAGE 18)

INGREDIENTS:
- **Tuna** — 2 small cans (or 1 family-size can)
- **Celery** — 1 cup — chopped up fine
- **Lemon juice** — ½ teaspoon
- **Mayonnaise** — ½ cup
- **Hard-boiled eggs** — 1 or 2, chopped up.

Wash celery stalks individually, under running water. As you cut off ends of stalks, try to remove the biggest strings. THEN CHOP CELERY INTO TINY HUNKS & DROP INTO LARGE MIXING BOWL.

Separate tuna with fork as you dig it out of can and drop into bowl. ADD LEMON JUICE & MAYONN. until it's consistency you like. ADD EGGS AND STIR UP.

VARIATIONS:
Add small amount of pickles (chopped up) — dill or sweet — and maybe even onions, or cucumbers.

GREAT FOR SANDWICHES

Here's What You Need

TO COOK AND SERVE A ROAST

- <u>Roast beef</u> or <u>leg of lamb</u>.

- <u>Roasting rack</u> (I hope it's Teflon).

- <u>Big oven pan</u> (to put rack in, and to catch grease that leaks through foil).

- <u>Aluminum foil</u> to line bottom of pan (and to wrap roast in, when you're ready to put leftovers in refrigerator or freezer). With foil, there will be no food stuck to pan. Hot water, liquid detergent and a Fuller vegetable brush will get pan clean after your pour out grease (into a can; see below) and throw foil away.

- <u>Old can or cottage cheese carton</u> for grease. Put it in refrigerator till it hardens, then throw it out with garbage. *Follow hint below first, if you wanna.*

- <u>Meat thermometer</u>.

- <u>Carving knife and fork</u>.

- <u>Booklet on "How to Carve."</u>

- <u>Platter to serve roast on</u>.

  OPTIONAL: Bacon (a luxury).

*HINT: After the grease hardens, turn can upside down and remove that end also and you'll find some jelly-like beef or lamb stock which you can save in refrig. or freezer for gravy, stew, or soup.

Roast Beef or Lamb

① <u>Set oven at 350°</u>.

② <u>Line roasting pan with foil</u>. OPTIONAL: If you have bacon, drape a couple of pieces over the top of roast. No need to season, in any case.

③ <u>Insert thermometer in roast</u>. (Read directions that come with thermometer.)

④ <u>Put meat on rack</u> (fat side up) in pan lined with foil.

⑤ <u>Put whole works in oven</u>.

YOU CAN'T HURT GOOD MEAT EXCEPT BY OVERCOOKING.

RULE OF THUMB:

Roast beef: Cook 18 to 20 min. per lb.

Leg of lamb: Cook 30 min. to the pound.

The best buys are huge roasts of heavy beef. They stretch far, have little waste (if they are sirloin or rib roasts); they taste great, and make wonderful leftover meals. SLICE THIN.

LEFTOVER SUGGESTIONS:

<u>Cold sliced meat</u> (plain or for sandwiches)
<u>Stew</u> (p. 19)
<u>Meat hunks over rice</u> (using brown gravy mix.)

HOW TO BROIL STEAKS

Select 1" thick steaks, if possible. Take meat out of refrigerator an hour before cooking, if you have time. Open the package and cut off all but a tiny edge of the fat. (Note: After the steak is in the oven, be sure to wash the counter top where it may have leaked juices.)

① Line pan with foil.

② Lay steaks on foil.

③ Optional: Shake a little SOY SAUCE on top of steaks.

④ (If you don't have a separate broiler on your stove): Place oven shelf 6" or less from top heating unit.

⑤ Set stove at "BROIL".

⑥ Leave oven door (or broiler door) cracked open.

⑦ Cook 3 min. on each side

If steak is too rare, drop to next lower rack in oven and cook one minute (or longer) on each side.

Every stove (gas or electric) varies, so experiment a little. You can always put a steak back for more cooking, so

DON'T OVERCOOK!

TURKEY

The greatest bargain in the meat world is a 20-pound Tom Turkey, if you can buy one around Thanksgiving or Christmas vacation time that hasn't been frozen. (I don't care what they say - freezing a turkey takes away flavor.)

It is an absolute cinch to cook it in foil, according to the directions included in every box of Reynolds Aluminum Foil, (heavy duty).

The turkey is roasted in a very hot oven -450°- wrapped in heavy duty foil as directed. This even eliminates having a nasty pan to scrub with Brillo!

A 20-pound turkey takes from 3-1/4 to 3-½ hours of cooking, **unstuffed**. (And don't waste your time stuffing it. Buy Pepperidge Farm stuffing mix and follow their simple directions. Cook stuffing in a separate pan when it's convenient. Takes almost no time.)

You can eat cold sliced turkey (or put it in sandwiches) happily for days -- and the leftovers are delicious in all the same recipes you used for chicken.

Do wash your turkey (especially the inside cavity) under running water before cooking.

Always be careful about keeping fowl (cooked or uncooked) refrigerated.

A FOIL-COOKED TURKEY IS NOT AS BEAUTIFULLY, EVENLY BROWNED AS THE TIME-CONSUMING TYPE, BUT IT TASTES JUST AS GREAT.

ONE-DISH MeaL
for 4
"MEAT CHOWDER"

① Put: 1 Tablesp. Corn oil in big skillet — on MED. HEAT

② Add: at least 1 lb. lean Ground Beef (ROUND or CHUCK) — if you can afford it.

③ SPRINKLE WITH SALT & A TEENY BIT OF GARLIC SALT
Cook till barely done and pour off grease
Hint: save old cartons or cans for this. Pour grease into them, harden in refrig., then discard

④ Dump in:
   1 Med. size Can of Tomatoes
   ½ Chopped Onion (some like more)
   1 Pkg. frozen mixed vegetables
   (GREEN & LIMA BEANS, CARROTS, CORN, AND PEAS)

Cook gently for 30 minutes
(AFTER IT BOILS, TURN TO LOWEST HEAT)

⑤ Then add:
   1 Can Franco-American Macaroni
   or Fr-Amer. Spaghetti & cheese
   (LARGE CAN)

THAT'S IT! Additional grated cheese optional.

SERVE WITH HOT LOAF OF PULL-APART BREAD OR BROWN 'N' SERVE ROLLS.

TUNA, HAM OR CHICKEN MAY BE SUBSTITUTED FOR THE GROUND BEEF.

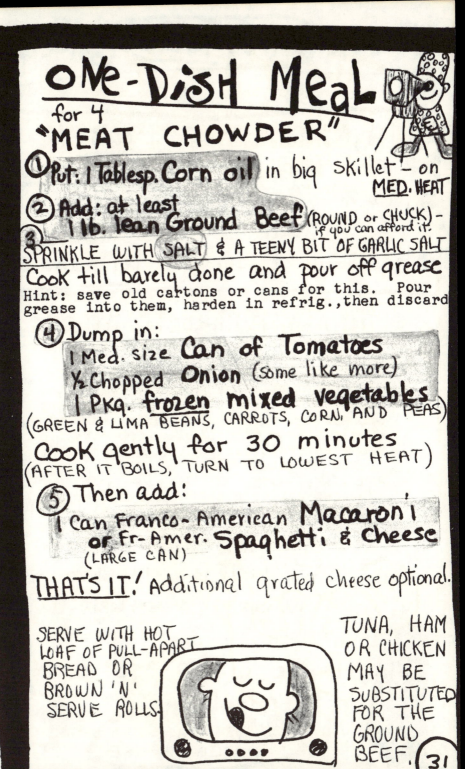

QUICK VEGETABLE CASSEROLE

Serves 4 - 8

- 1 large can of tiny **peas**
- 2 med. cans of **green asparagus**
- 1 can of **mushroom** or **cheddar cheese soup**
- handful of cut-up **almonds**

OPTIONAL: MUSHROOM PIECES. Drain liquid off peas & asparagus. Cover bottom of casserole with peas, then a layer of asparagus, then squish on a layer of undiluted soup. (Sprinkle almonds over this, if you use them.) REPEAT LAYERS. Mushrooms or almonds (or crushed cornflakes!) on top. Bake in 300°-350° oven 30 minutes.

HINT: YOU CAN ALWAYS ADD GRATED CHEESE

Green Beans

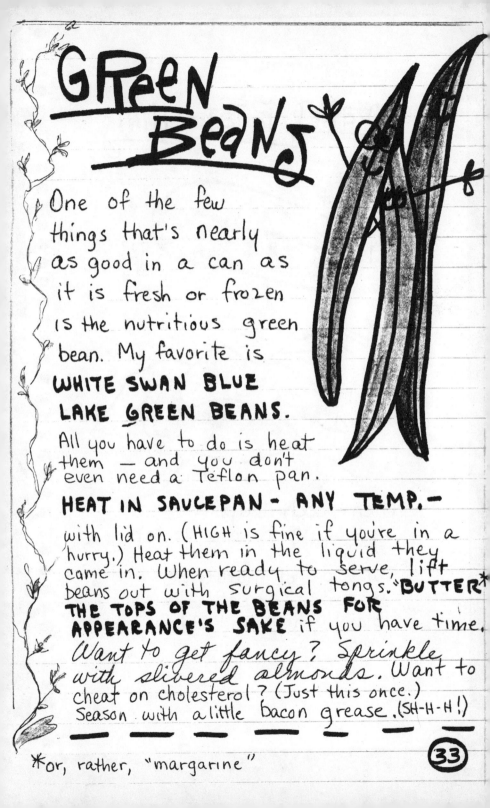

One of the few things that's nearly as good in a can as it is fresh or frozen is the nutritious green bean. My favorite is **WHITE SWAN BLUE LAKE GREEN BEANS.**

All you have to do is heat them — and you don't even need a Teflon pan.

HEAT IN SAUCEPAN - ANY TEMP. — with lid on. (HIGH is fine if you're in a hurry.) Heat them in the liquid they came in. When ready to serve, lift beans out with surgical tongs. **"BUTTER*** **THE TOPS OF THE BEANS FOR APPEARANCE'S SAKE** if you have time. Want to get fancy? Sprinkle with slivered almonds. Want to cheat on cholesterol? (Just this once.) Season with a little bacon grease. (SH-H-H!)

---

*or, rather, "margarine"

(33)

Baked Potato Hints

When done, punch with a fork thusly:

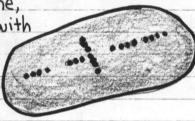

TOP VIEW OF POTATO

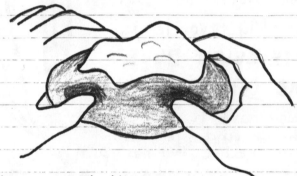

Then pooch it up, squeezing toward center.

Put a pat of margarine in center. Great with plain yogurt and chives, too.

Baked Potatoes

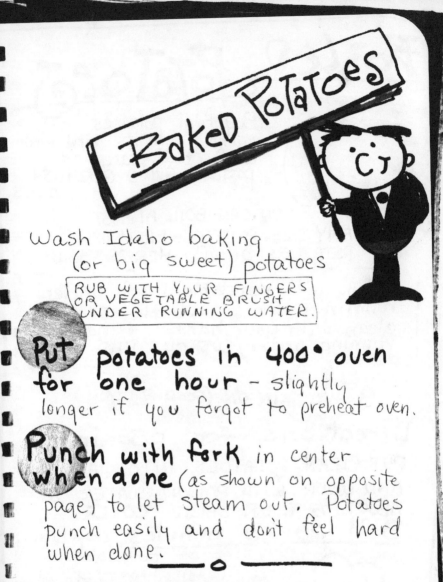

Wash Idaho baking (or big sweet) potatoes

RUB WITH YOUR FINGERS OR VEGETABLE BRUSH UNDER RUNNING WATER.

Put potatoes in 400° oven for one hour — slightly longer if you forgot to preheat oven.

Punch with fork when done in center (as shown on opposite page) to let steam out. Potatoes punch easily and don't feel hard when done.

―――○―――

GOOD IDEA: Bake several extra for use 2 or 3 days later. Don't punch when done — just stick in refrigerator. When you need 'em, peel and cut up and reheat in cheese soup — or dice and brown in oil in frying pan (HASH BROWNED.) Add salt and pepper.

35

Boiled Potatoes

Buy firm potatoes without sprouts and with as few bad places as possible. AVOID GREENISH ONES.

YOU CAN BOIL ALMOST ANY SIZE POTATO - FROM NEW POTATOES ON UP. HERE'S HOW:

Scrub with vegetable brush under running water (or rub the skins clean with your hands — under running water.) CUT OUT BAD SPOTS.

LEAVE SKIN ON. (GOOD FOR YOU.)

Directions for cooking:

PUT CLEAN POTATOES INTO PAN AND COVER WITH BOILING WATER & ABOUT ½ TEASP. SALT. **COVER.**

Boil 20-60 minutes depending upon size of potatoes.

They're done if tender when stuck with a fork. DRAIN ON PAPER TOWEL

Serve with margarine melting on top.

IN A HURRY? CUT POTATOES IN ¼THS BEFORE COOKING

BING CHERRY MOLDED SALAD
MAKE-AHEAD

Drain:
2 (1 lb.) cans {PITTED} **DARK SWEET (OR BING) CHERRIES** and place in bottom of ring mold

• • • • • • • • • • • •

INTO BIG PYREX MEASURING JAR, EMPTY:

1 (3 oz.) envelope **BLACK CHERRY JELLO**

into: 1½ cups (or less) **BOILING WATER.** Stir!

ADD: 2 Tablespoons of **BOURBON** (IF YOU'RE 21 OR OVER)

POUR THIS MIXTURE OVER CHERRIES (IN MOLD)

Cover with wax paper and refrigerate at least 6 hours. (Or in freezer if you're in a hurry, for much shorter time. BUT WATCH IT!) (DON'T LET IT FREEZE.)

UNMOLD & SERVE AS SHOWN

SURROUND WITH WASHED LETTUCE

FILL WITH DRESSING

TO UNMOLD:
Turn mold upside down on plate or platter and rub a hot, wet (CLEAN!) washcloth around the outside bottom of ring mold until it drops free. Judicious use of a knife will help.

DRESSING ON NEXT PAGE
(over)

Peach, Pineapple or Pear & Cheese Salad

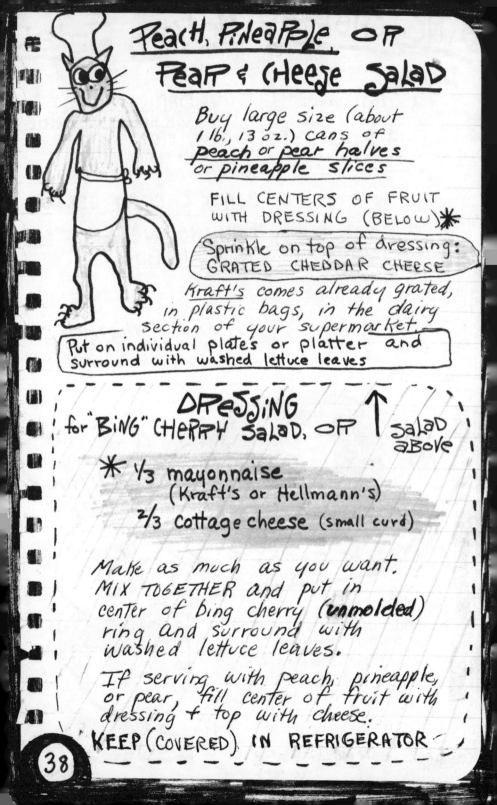

Buy large size (about 1 lb., 13 oz.) cans of **peach** or **pear** halves or **pineapple** slices

FILL CENTERS OF FRUIT WITH DRESSING (BELOW) ✶

Sprinkle on top of dressing: GRATED CHEDDAR CHEESE

Kraft's comes already grated, in plastic bags, in the dairy section of your supermarket.

Put on individual plates or platter and surround with washed lettuce leaves

Dressing
for "BING" CHERRY SALAD, OR ↑ salad above

✶ 1/3 mayonnaise (Kraft's or Hellmann's)

2/3 cottage cheese (small curd)

Make as much as you want. MIX TOGETHER and put in center of bing cherry **(unmolded)** ring and surround with washed lettuce leaves.

If serving with peach, pineapple, or pear, fill center of fruit with dressing & top with cheese.

KEEP (COVERED) IN REFRIGERATOR

38

Tossed "Green" Salad

1. Put (lemon juice, corn oil, and salt (GOOD SEASONS SALAD DRESSING OR — SEE OPPOSITE PAGE) in bottom of big mixing bowl or salad bowl.

2. ADD any or all: (wash + cut up)
   - Tomatoes
   - Celery
   - Cucumbers
   - Avocado slices
   - Carrot slices
   - Green pepper "
   - etc.

3. Toss these vegetables in the dressing.

4. Lay washed, drained (or dried between paper towels) **lettuce** leaves BROKEN INTO BITE-SIZE PIECES **on top of the** dressing + **vegetables.** DO NOT TOSS FURTHER UNTIL READY TO EAT.

Cover bowl with plastic wrap and place in refrigerator so lettuce will be crisp at serving (+ tossing) time.

DO WASH ALL LETTUCE CAREFULLY UNDER RUNNING WATER. DRAIN IN COLANDER.

Store in plastic bag with paper towels in bottom in refrig.

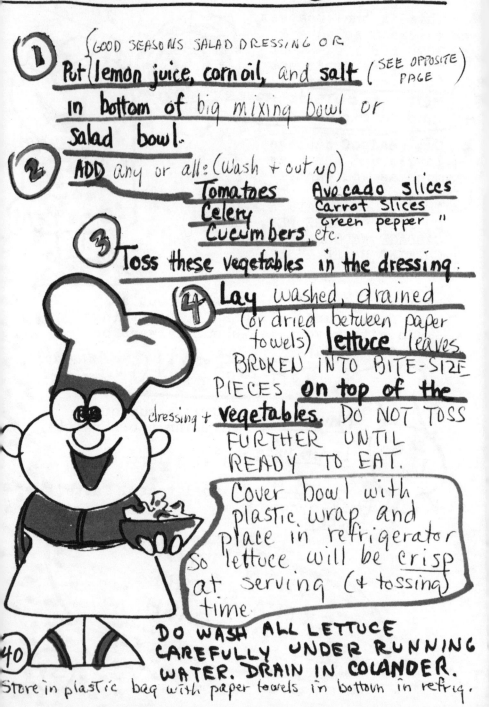

40

Quick Ambrosia

In the bottom of a bowl, thaw:

2 Tablesp. (OR MORE) <u>frozen orange juice</u>, undiluted

Into that, toss until coated with the juice:

1 or more fresh, sliced <u>bananas</u>

Stir in:

1 can (16 oz.) Libby's <u>Lite Fruit Cocktail</u>, DRAINED, but save the juice and drink it. It's all fruit juice; no sugar added.

<u>Optional:</u>

Add diced, fresh (scrubbed) apples, with peels (TOSS APPLES IN O.J. SO THEY WON'T CHANGE COLOR) and/or any fresh fruit on hand, cut up and/or chopped pecans

Easy PORK CHOPS & Rice

① COMBINE IN BUTTERED CASSEROLE:

- Small pkg. (7 oz.) MINUTE RICE
- ½ envelope Lipton's ONION SOUP MIX
- Can of undiluted CREAM OF CHICKEN (OR CELERY) SOUP
- 1½ cups BOILING WATER

You need 4 or more PORK CHOPS

② → Brown chops lightly in oiled skillet.
③ → Season with salt and pepper.
④ → Put on top of rice mixture.
⑤ → Bake, covered, in 375° oven for about 1 hr., 15 min.

CHICKEN PIECES MAY BE SUBSTITUTED!

GOOD WITH IT:
Halved avocados brushed with lemon juice and filled with canned Mandarin orange sections.

PORK 'N' BEANS

CHOP UP: 1/2 green pepper (or use equivalent of frozen, chopped)

OPEN: 1 large can Campbell's Pork & Beans and put contents in casserole with green peppers

STIR IN:
- 1 - 2 Tablespoons syrup (any kind)
- 1/8 teaspoon onion salt
- 1/2 teaspoon dry mustard (if you have it)
- 1/8 teaspoon salt
- 1/4 teaspoon Worcestershire Sauce
- 1 Tablespoon ketchup
- 1 Tablespoon (liquid) coffee (if you have it; cold or hot)

Bacon may be draped across top.

BAKE 45 MINUTES OR MORE AT 275°.
There are infinite varieties of this. Add chopped hot dogs or ham to make it a meal.

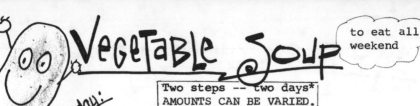

Vegetable Soup

to eat all weekend

Two steps -- two days*
AMOUNTS CAN BE VARIED.

1st day:

Into a big pot put:

2 big **SOUP BONES** into cold, lightly salted **WATER** (almost any amount; just be sure water covers bones, from whence cometh the flavor). Bring to boil.

ADD: 1 can (14½ oz.) **STEWED TOMATOES**.

Bring to a boil *again*, and cover. Simmer several hours at least. The longer the better. Add water if needed.

PUT PAN AND ALL IN REFRIGERATOR OVERNIGHT.

2nd day: Remove solidified fat layer from soup

and discard. (NOT down the sink! The hardened grease (cholesterol!) can be disposed of in an old grocery sack, plastic bag, or can. Give soup bones to deserving dog owner. Then ADD:

1 lb. cut-up <u>stew meat</u> (no fat)

to the cold water. BRING WATER TO BOIL and ADD:

pkg. frozen <u>soup vegetables</u> or mixed vegs.
a couple of whole <u>bay leaves</u> (Remove before serving.)
1 chopped <u>onion</u> (frozen O.K.) OR ONION SALT
2 or more <u>potatoes</u>, peeled, cut up

and any leftover veggies or meat on hand. (I freeze and save even tiny amounts of leftover vegetables and all the water they were cooked in -- even canned veggies -- and add these frozen blobs to the soup.)

Simmer, covered, a couple of hours or more.

Need to stretch leftover soup? Add canned V-8 (any amount).

*In a hurry? Can't take two days? Boil bones and tomatoes several hours, then blot fat off top of liquid with paper towels. After all fat is gone, proceed as directed above.

44

FIRST SHOPPING LIST and

KEEP-iN STOCK LisT

- Olive oil (best for you) and other cooking oil (Wesson, etc.)
- → Flour - 2 lb. sack, enriched, all-purpose
- Sugar (but don't use much!)
- → Bisquick - small box for muffins, pancakes, waffles
- Syrup (for your NutriGrain whole grain waffles)
- → Minute Rice - huge size
- Slivered almonds - can or package
- → Box of peppercorns - for grinder
- Salt - iodized - or Morton's "Lite Salt"
- → Paprika - smallest size
- Onion powder and garlic powder
- → Package of beef gravy mix
- Bottle of Lite Italian Salad Dressing
- → Shaker of Parmesan cheese
- Soy sauce
- → Cereals - whole grain
- Bread - whole wheat (2 loaves -- 1 for freezer compartment)
- → Bran - oat and also wheat bran, natural, unprocessed
- Soups - Cream of mushroom, cream of chicken, cheddar cheese
- → Green beans + green peas (young, tender) ← 2 of each
- Canned LITE fruit: peaches, pear, pineapple, fruit cocktail
- → Ranch Style Beans
- Peanut butter - natural (nothing added)
- → Honey (Try peanut butter and honey sandwiches)
- Tuna - family size, solid-packed in water
- → Raisins
- Liquid detergent (also dishwasher detergent, if needed)
- → Bars of soap (Keep one in the kitchen!)
- Brillo soap pads (or Tuffy for Teflon & Silverstone)
- → Paper towels
- Paper napkins

Of course you don't need to buy everything on this list, but you are prepared for almost any kitchen emergency if you do!

(more)

Keep-in-Refrigerator List

- <u>Milk</u> - skim or low-fat
- → <u>Eggs</u> - throw yolks (yellow part) away when possible. In recipes, substitute 2 egg whites for "1 egg". (See inside of front cover.)
- <u>Margarine</u>
- → <u>Lite mayonnaise</u>
- <u>Celery</u>, <u>carrots</u>, <u>green peppers</u>
- → <u>Lettuce</u> and <u>tomatoes</u>
- <u>Parmesan cheese</u>

Keep-in-Freezer Compartment

- Frozen <u>orange juice</u>
- → Frozen <u>chopped onions</u>
- 2 lbs. <u>lean ground beef</u>
- → Extra loaf of <u>whole grain bread</u>
- "<u>Egg Beaters</u> with Cheez"
- → Whole grain <u>Nutri Grain waffles</u>
- Frozen <u>vegetables</u>
- → <u>Lean Cuisine</u> entrées

46

QUICK 'N' DIFFERENT

Finger Foods and Dips

Delicate + unusual → Cut <u>toast</u> into tiny squares. On each, spread on a small dab of lite mayonnaise. TOP WITH: tiny single ring of sliced <u>onion. Run under broiler before serving.</u>

Full of Vit. C and crunchy → Wash and cut <u>green peppers</u> into long sections about 2 inches wide. (Remove seeds and pulp.) Spread low-fat <u>cream cheese</u> on these strips. Sprinkle with salt. (Morton's Lite preferred.)

AVOCADO DIP:

Sensational! → Peel and mash ripe avocado (in bowl) with fork. Mix with desired amount of plain yogurt. Salt to taste. → Great with Triscuit.

Super easy → QUICK, but not so different: Surely you already know about "California Dip". All it takes is a small package of Lipton's Onion Soup Mix and 8 oz. plain yogurt (instead of sour cream) mixed together. That's all. Serve with whole grain corn chips.

(SUPER!) <u>ARTICHOKE BLENDER DIP</u>

Too good to be true → Put in blender: one regular size can of artichoke hearts (drained), along with one cup Parmesan cheese, and one cup of lite mayonnaise. That's all! Blend and heat in oven dish in 350 degree oven for 20-25 minutes. It will be a big hit.
any kind of crackers

Refrigerate anything with eggs, mayonnaise, or dairy products. Cover with Saran wrap.

—Reprinted by permission—

Chances are, you eat like someone who doesn't think they could get cancer.

The next time you sit down to a cheeseburger, fries and soft drink, pretend you're the other guy.

A lot of people eat like they don't believe a word about cancer-causing foods and substances.

Well, take heed. Because there is now a good deal of evidence that poor dietary habits contribute to the risk of cancer. Some experts suggest that 40% of all cancer in men and 60% of all cancer in women is nutrition-linked. And we're not talking about the other guy. We're talking about you.

At Moncrief Radiation Center, we believe the evidence is strong enough to offer you some healthy advice about the anti-cancer diet. 1. Eat less fat. 2. Eat more high-fiber foods like fruit, vegetables and whole grains. 3. Eat foods rich in Vitamins A and C. 4. Eat "cruciferous" vegetables like broccoli, cauliflower and cabbage. 5. Avoid alcohol. 6. Use less salt.

We've been treating cancer patients effectively at Moncrief for more than 28 years. So if you have some questions concerning nutrition, maybe our oncology dietitian can provide the answers over the phone.

The way we see it, we all have to live with cancer's threat.

But nobody said we can't decrease the risk.

THE WM. A. & ELIZABETH B.
MONCRIEF
RADIATION CENTER
1450 Eighth Avenue
Fort Worth, Texas 76104
(817) 923-7393

TARRANT COUNTY PHYSICIAN